Fearless

MATEJA MITCHELL

Fearless

© 2017 Mateja Mitchell

FearlessWeStand.com

Cover image credit: © Jakub Gojda

Published by: Austin Startup School

AustinStartUpSchool.com

ISBN: 0-9990182-0-5

ISBN-13: 978-0-9990182-0-0

DEDICATION

To mom~ I love you to the moon and back! You were here with me in these hard times and I'm so grateful for you! You made my life a million times easier, and I don't know what I'd do without you.

You bring out the sides of me people should know. You have made me a better person. You encouraged me to write this book and now here I am a published author and a fearless young girl. I wouldn't be here without you.

So, thanks mama.

CONTENTS

ACKNOWLEDGMENTS

Thank you to Ben & Suzanne and everyone at
Austin StartUp School who helped guide me through this
writing process and helped me to
unleash my fearless voice!

I appreciate your help so much, and wouldn't have been
able to publish this book without you!

THE BEGINNING

Fear.

We all have it... I have it. It's really tough when you're so afraid. You feel like you're all cornered and all you can do is give up all hope, but that's why I'm here. I'm writing this book for that very reason. I've felt so many bad things. I tried to do all the things I thought would help, but they didn't. So let me share some things I really think helped me and could help you.

Let's start simple. Hi, I'm Mateja Mitchell. I'm the oldest of five kids and a great help to my loving parents. I'm a young girl and just starting real big "adult life" you could say, and this is my book. I just want to start off by saying, wow. I mean all of this happened by support and a lot of work, but we're finally here. So enjoy.

When I was younger, let's say about toddler to third grade, I was fearless. Never a doubt in the world. Life was just, well, perfect. I loved my sister and parents, I had my aunt and grandma living with us, and they were the best. I cared for them so much and hoped they'd never leave.

1

A few years passed and I found out my aunt was moving to China. She was my best friend, and I was devastated. I wished her good luck, we said our goodbyes and she was gone. Just like that. I was so sad, but at least now I still have my grammy, right?

Nope! Life had other plans. My grandma was moving to Thailand!

WHAT?!? How could this be happening? I lost two people I really cared about. Right here in my life was where fear really came in for the first time. I was scared I was going to lose my parents and anyone else I cared about!

After a while I felt much better. My mom decided to be a stay at home mom, so that really helped. I started feeling more comfortable with my aunt and grandma being gone. Then we moved into this beautiful home, and soon after my little sister Hava was born. I loved her with all my heart. She was a special one, hahaha. Everything was great, but we know life isn't perfect, so it threw its next challenge at us. My dad lost his job.

At first it was no big deal and everything seemed normal. That didn't last! Suddenly we were on a tight tight budget. We couldn't go out to eat anymore, we couldn't go to movies, or do almost anything that cost money. I was so scared we would lose our house, and it would just get worse.

One day though, a window opened. My dad got a job! I was overfilled with joy! We weren't going to be homeless! Everything was going to be okay! Thank you Jesus! Or so I thought...

MOVING

A year after my dad got that job, everything was great. He loved his new company and we weren't homeless. But then one day my parents told us we were moving to a place far from where I grew up...Redding, California.

I stormed to my room, slammed the door and wept. I cried and cried, and being as young as I was, I wanted to never come out again.

Eventually, maybe two hours later, I returned and asked *why* we were moving. I mean it's perfect here, right? Everything we need is right here!
My mother explained to me why we had to move, and she told me we would buy animals, land, a nice big house, and settle for a while. It was always a dream of mine to own animals, so it eased the pain a little.

Of course now I had to face the fact I had to tell my best friends we were leaving. One of the hardest things was that one of my best friends told me about a month before that she was moving right down the street, so we could see each other all the time. Not anymore.

3

I was devastated, but what could I do about it? Crying wouldn't help, it would just waste time and energy. So I had to trust them and try to understand why my parents would do this. Yeah, I guess I'd just have to trust them.

A few months passed and all of my friends said their goodbyes, and finally…moving day was here. I was so nervous and scared of what was to come. We started driving and it was four hours long, but we finally got there.

I really liked the house, so that helped, and I just went to bed so I could start the next day. The next day flew by, unpacking and getting used to the house, and I met a friend which was very exciting. And who knew that girl I met would become one of my best friends! Yay meeee!

Several days went by while I was busy unpacking and school shopping. I didn't realize at the time that school would start exactly three weeks after we moved in! "Hopefully I'll make friends and do well," I thought. "I mean how hard can it be?"

SCHOOL'S SURPRISES

Finally it was here. The first day of public school, EVER. Prior to this I had only been homeschooled. I was excited and nervous at the same time. I was starting fourth grade! Go me! I felt even proud in a way.

Then I found out I had to ride the bus...I had never ridden a bus before! This felt scary. Then I began to wonder what else would feel scary. There could be mean kids, bullies, a mean teacher, who knows! All this doubt just started pouring in my mind.

I was so scared!

Why was I so afraid? I was letting fear control me, but why? At that time I didn't know the answer to this. Heck, I barely knew what fear was.

As the day went on there were so many crazy things that happened. First, when I started school I knew no bad words. That changed on day one. I didn't know people were allowed to keep guns or weapons out in the open.

That changed too. And, I had no idea people could come into your house and steal things, also known as robbery!

That actually happened!

I mean if I didn't have the comfort of my mother to be there for me, I do not know what could have happened. I might have lost my mind. And the scary thing was, this was only day one. Who knows what could happen now. I was terrified.

How could I be sure I would be safe? What could I do? I pondered, and was confused. How am I going to live my life like this? Should I even continue? What horrible things are coming in my future? My life has changed, *forever.*

I know this sounds crazy to believe or like I'm being dramatic, but it's true. I never thought there would be so much hate and negativity in this world, but public school opened up a new door for me.

I didn't realize how big of a door this was...

REDDING'S PATHS

It had been a couple of months. I had gotten used to school, but I was not happy about the situation at all. I wished I could just quit school and forget all this yuck I was inhaling every day. I mean, the amount of sexual content I heard about everyday disgusted me.

I was also boiling at the thought of my sister hearing all of this, and the extent that she was being bullied about how she couldn't read, or had a bit of a different personality from the rest. I was sick of it all. Why should I have to be stuck in the middle of this? Why was this all happening to me? Was it all really worth it?

Real suicidal thoughts came to my mind sometimes. But, I knew better. Push those thoughts out and think of the positive! Start dancing for joy that you have such awesome friends, and a wonderful family. I told myself this all the time when I was feeling down.

In school I had the best teacher ever! She was kind, and I was the teacher's pet you could say.
I loved her, and this was amazing because it helped with

the fear and feelings I didn't want, so much.

Then one day around Valentine's Day I was outside with my sister Arielle, the second eldest, taking our baby sister out for a walk in the stroller. We were having so much fun, but I looked down and realized Arielle was kind of coming in close, and before I knew what was really happening she tripped me and fell on top of me!

I face-planted into the street and blacked out. When I came to, I was so confused but realized that somehow I had pushed the stroller and my baby sister safely to the sidewalk. My face hurt so bad! I put my hand over my cheek where it hurt most. I took it off and my hand was covered in blood. I couldn't seem to get on my feet, then I looked ahead and saw that a huge UPS truck was coming my way! I was petrified. Was this the end?

I looked around and saw Arielle run inside the house with all of the color drained from her face. The next thing I know my mother was running out of the house. A look of relief came over her when she saw me. She stopped the truck and carried me inside, and gently laid me on the couch.

"Mommy," I said. "Why did you look better when you saw me?"
"I thought you had been hit by a car, from the look on your sister's face."
"Oh," I softly whispered.

I felt so tired I could barely move. My mom quickly brought me a warm washcloth. I placed it on my face and quietly lay there wanting to just drift to sleep, but my mom told me I needed to stay awake, I could have a concussion. So I lay there, wondering how was I supposed to go to school like this?

I got up to see myself in the mirror. As soon as my eyes met the glass, I wept. The whole left side of my face was raw skin. I was horrified. I looked like a monster. I'm not going to school ever again, I thought. I cried to my mom, and begged her to let me stay home the next day. Of course she said yes. I felt so much better now that I could stay - I couldn't imagine going to school looking like this! All I could do was weep.

Eventually my head hurt so bad from hitting it and crying, I decided there was no good to keep crying. So I laid in my bed and drifted off to sleep while my mom checked on me through the night.

The next day went easy. I rested, and my mom cleaned up my scraped face. And oh boy did it hurt. It felt like a million little bees were stinging my face. It was awful.

Later that day my dad came home and explained to me that he had told my teacher what had happened, and how I felt embarrassed about my face. So my teacher decided to tell the class if they made fun of me at all, they would get a pink slip. I felt so treasured! People really do care. Wow. People care, ask if you need help. People really do care.

On Valentine's day my mom put a huge bandage on my face with two little hearts..it looked ridiculous. I came to school, still nervous about my face, wondering what those kids were going to say. I was shocked when I found out.

When I walked into class everyone stared, and then out of nowhere, they cheered. I was so shocked I didn't realize I was smiling. I sat down at my usual place, blushing. I was so happy. At lunch everyone was complimenting my face! Like.... What!? I didn't understand the compassion people really can have.

At recess I looked and saw my little sister all by herself. I walked over and asked her what the matter was. Of course, a girl was making fun of her, about how she couldn't read. So I walked over to that girl, and I had to remember to remain calm and not start screaming at her.

So I peacefully told her it was very, very unkind to treat people that way. So please stop. She kind of gave me this look like, who do you think you are? And rolled her eyes. I stayed calm, well on the outside, and said "Sass isn't going to help your case, plus I could easily tell your teacher what you've been up to."

"Well then you'll be a tattle tale and I'll tell everybody!" she said.

I looked at her like, seriously? I didn't care if she told the whole world who I was. I know the truth, and that's what matters. So I looked at her one more time and without another word I left. I think she got the idea, because she left my little sister alone the rest of the day.

Confront your bullies or tell others. Research shows ninety-five percent of bullies who've been confronted, stop. So make a difference. Don't be a bystander who watches kids, girls, or people in general get bullied.

It can really help to share and put a BIG stop to bullying.

It's a real issue all over America. And sadly research shows that adults who were bullied as children, become the bullies as adults. And in some of the worst cases they become the shooters at schools.

HALLOWEEN'S HORRORS

A month before Halloween my parents said they had something to tell me. I was just kinda like, "Ok, what's up?" Then out of nowhere, "We are moving to Texas, and driving across the country to get there. So we will need to leave in a couple of weeks".

I blurted back with "WHAT!? We can't move! Maddie and I have huge plans for Halloween! I'm not going! We just got here! It's only been one year!"

I was burning with anger. All I wanted to do was scream my head off, but I remained calm, well on the outside at least. I ran to my room, crying. How many times were we going to have to keep moving? Was I ever going to have any real friends? All I could do was cry.

The next day I begged my mother for us not to move, but she did make some great points as to why we were moving. My dad was always gone. He traveled all the time. I really missed him. So I decided to suck it up and move with a good attitude. I mean what choice did I have? Oh right, none.

The next day I told the horrible news to my friends. I invited them over and we talked for hours. Everything felt a whole lot better after we had talked. Although, this didn't change the fact that the news physically hurt. It felt like my heart had just been beat hundreds of times. I mean moving four hours away last year sucked, but at least I could visit.

Not this time. Was I even going to make any friends? I had to stop thinking this way, because it was tearing me up. I needed to clear my head and just make the most of the time I had left.

LONE STAR STATE

It was finally here. We were moving to Texas. I was in disbelief.
Another terrible thing I was angry at was that my dad couldn't even leave with us. We were leaving so late at night, and my dad was staying in Redding, and wouldn't leave until a couple of days later.

Why should I have to leave if he didn't have to? Life's unfair, and I needed to realize it. All I could do was think of all the negative things about this move. Like I had to drive across this country with all of my little sisters?! We'll probably never get there with these kids. Ugh, I was so furious. There will be little kids screaming and all I can do is sit there and be in the mix...although I knew deep down we would get there.

After a long three weeks, we made it. I was an official resident of Texas. It was really crazy to think about, and I really wished all my friends were with me, but I had to keep positive thoughts and move on.

BLUEBONNETS

School started about two weeks after we arrived in Texas.
My mom decided to put me into a private school.
I was like, NOOO! I did not want to be put in school.
I wanted to be homeschooled.

I begged my mom, but she had already enrolled me.

Ugh.

Well, I might as well. What else did I have to lose? Plus I had no friends and wasn't going to make any unless I put myself out there.

So, again, there was no point in complaining.

I told myself, "you can do all things you put your mind to. You got this, girl".

SCHOOL PREP

About a week before school I started a day camp to get prepared. On the first day I was late. Of course just what I needed, unwanted attention. I sat in the back, quieter than the smallest bug in the world. I had my head down, looking at the floor. Only looking up every once in a while.

After a few teachers had taken turns speaking, I glanced up again, but this time it was different. When I looked up there was this one girl who stood out. For example, it was like there were all of these blues, and one red. She didn't even have anything bold on, and the weirdest part was I couldn't see her face. I only saw the back of her head. I got this, almost like a vision, that we were going to be best friends and I was going to have a ton of friends. I was like... okay. What just happened? I was so confused. I just listened and kept quiet.

Soon it was lunch time and I just walked past her staring. She looked at me and I quickly put my eyes to the floor, trying not to make eye contact. I don't even really understand why I was so scared to talk to her. I mean I had just had this thought we were going to be friends. So why didn't I go talk to her? I'll tell you why: Fear. It's just that simple. I was letting that emotion control me. It needed to stop. And it wouldn't unless I put the work into it. Which I didn't. I kept letting it take control of me.

Later at lunch she walked over and just said hi, and told me her name was Audrey. That's about all it took. Soon we were talking so much it was like we had known each other for years.

An hour later it was time for games. So they put us in random groups. I was crossing my fingers that I would get to be with Audrey. After all, she was the only person I knew. Life doesn't work that way though. I got paired up with two girls my age and a counselor. One of the girls was named Blaire and the other was named Cammie. They were both so nice to me. I really liked hanging out with them. We played a couple of games, but we didn't win. I didn't care though. I had made new friends and I was so happy.

After the games were over Blaire invited me to go meet one of her friends. I was hesitant at first, but I knew if I didn't go I could lose an opportunity to meet new people. So I went, and I met her friend Christine. She was so nice and really upbeat. She loved the color pink, which I thought was so bold of her. I mean you don't meet that many people who say, "My favorite color's pink!" nowadays. I used to say that in fourth grade and got picked on. So I kinda dropped pink and moved on with other colors.

So anyways, she was great. She wanted to introduce me to a group of girls. I didn't hesitate this time and just went for it. They were all nice, but one of them seemed a little upset at first - her name was Hannah - but she came around. I asked the girls why she seemed to be upset, and they just said she was kind of worried about change.

It turns out these girls had been friends since pre-K. I felt worry come over me like a giant wave just crashed down. I kept thinking that they wouldn't want to hang out with me because I was new and they'd known each other for years. I had to stop all this nonsense with fear and paranoia. It was breaking me.

The day went on and Christine told me about a group chat they had and she wanted to add me on. I felt that wave go down. I felt a lot better. I just had to give this time. I mean school hadn't even started yet and I already had friends!

SIXTH GRADE ISN'T EASY

School was starting today and I was so excited! I was so grateful for my friends that I didn't even think I would have when I moved. Wow, I had come this far...what other nice surprises did life have in store for me? I was so excited. So off to school I went!

The first day was simple, just getting warmed up and ready for school. The rest of the week was the same, no homework that was too difficult. So I got the hang of it. A month had passed and school was good.

So there was this girl Jewel, who I didn't know very well, but apparently she liked me. She was always around and really liked hanging with me. I didn't really want to be around her but I also didn't want to be mean so I let her hang out. But there was something I didn't know. Audrey and Jewel knew each other from the third grade!

I wondered, why wouldn't Audrey tell me? Does she not feel comfortable talking to me about personal things? Why wouldn't she? What was wrong with me?

Then I came to realize I needed to block out any bad thoughts that came to my mind, because this was getting out of hand and I was done. So I decided for any bad thoughts I might be getting to immediately tell myself something positive afterward.

Something along the lines of, I'm amazing, I'm beautiful, I'm never going to think badly of myself ever again! I am *fearless*! And let me tell you, it worked! I had never felt better. I felt like a whole new me. I could do anything I put my mind to. So now I needed to apply this to all things. Start making a change.

Now that I was more brave about how I felt I went straight to Jewel and asked for some space. Everyone needs it. Next I decided to make a list of anything I may or may not need to get through so I could start working toward my goals. I can't even begin to explain what that felt like to be able to not be scared of anything that may be coming my way.

I was better than ever, and so excited to start really living. So I ignored the fact that Jewel got mad at me for asking for space. She bothered me about it only once in a while, so it wasn't too bad. She did hurt my feelings a couple of times, but I needed to remember how I was trying to change, so I brushed it all off.

I got good grades and had a lot of awesome friends. So my life was great. I wasn't expecting anything bad to happen, and if it did I told myself I was ready for it. But I wasn't.

One day at recess, me and my friends were talking and a couple of them had to go to the restroom. So Audrey and I started walking toward the school, and behind us was Jewel. I could tell something was off. I just told myself to remain calm, and take deep breaths. I asked Audrey to go to the building and wait for me, and she went swiftly. Jewel came right up to me with her friend Veronica, and I just stood there waiting for them to say something. Only what I got was nothing like I was expecting.

Out of nowhere Jewel starting shouting at me on how I was so mean, and how I didn't like her and how I ruined her life. I stood there gawking in shock. She started crying, which didn't help at all. Then her friend Veronica started shouting at me.

I was just standing there while they were hurting me with their words. I just couldn't believe what I was hearing. I could feel the hot tears start filling my eyes and the anger and sadness rising so quickly. Right there I looked her in the eye and let it all out. I shouted so loud I didn't recognize the level of vocals I was using, but I didn't care.

I told her, How dare she? I was only nice to her throughout the year and she had the nerve to come up to me and treat me like that? I cried my heart out and told her she needed to leave me alone - this time, forever.

I was done being bullied and disrespected. Her friend started talking in an angry voice, but she told her to quit it. I heard the whistle to go inside. I ran so fast and tried to pull myself together. I went inside and asked my teacher if I could have a couple of minutes in the restroom. He said it was alright, and I went there and cried like I never had before.

I looked up and told myself how brilliant I was for doing that. I realized if I hadn't spoken my mind I'd probably be dealing with this for so much longer than I needed. Now she was finally stood up to.

After class I told my friends what happened. They were all shocked about the whole situation, and were so proud I stood up to her. They told me how she had always been so mean to so many girls, and I was the first one to talk to her about it.

I felt so proud and confident in myself. I was brave, and more self-assured than ever.

FRIENDSHIPS FALL

The year went on, and no more issues occurred. Everything was great, and I became a lot closer with Audrey and Hannah. We were the inseparable trio and did everything together. Even though we were so close, we didn't exclude any of our other friends. We all got along, but I was closest with those two.

The summer rolled around and we planned an epic summer only to find out I was going to California to visit friends and family the whole summer! I was so upset, but since I had decided to be a better person I got over it and went, no problem.

I explained to the girls my situation. They were so understanding and caring. I felt so comfortable telling the one thing that ruined our plans. They just kept taking me to the bright side of things. I was so blessed and happy to have them. They promised to keep me updated on everything that happened, and FaceTime multiple times a week. I gave them a big hug and went to start packing.

Then it was here, the day I was leaving. We left bright

and early so we could get a good start. We had a great time. Halfway into our vacation Audrey texted me saying she needed to talk to me. I FaceTimed her right away, because I could sense this wasn't good.

As soon as she answered she sobbed.

Her dark brown eyes seemed to pop from all the red of her crying. She was sobbing and could barely speak. I felt my spine shiver. I had no idea what had happened and was scared she had been hurt. She looked at me over the phone and told me, "Hannah and I are no longer friends".

"What!?" I screamed.

I couldn't wrap my head around why they weren't friends! They had just gotten back from camp together. How could they not be friends, was all I could keep thinking. I was in shock. Just a month before you couldn't do anything to separate us and now they wouldn't even speak to each other. I told Audrey I needed to talk to Hannah. So I quickly hung up and FaceTimed her.

When she answered I asked about a hundred questions. I couldn't understand. She was so quiet and kept her eyes glued to the ground. I saw tears flooding her eyes. I shut up instantly. My mind kept racing with thoughts. I looked at the floor and just kept wondering how this could've happened.

Then out of nowhere she spoke softly and told me she and Audrey got into a big fight at camp. My jaw dropped. It must've been a bad fight, I thought, because nothing could have separated us a month ago. She told me how it happened and I was sad and mad at the same time. It turns out a lot of girls that were my friends were involved. I cried with her.

I realized they weren't going to be talking again anytime soon.

So I needed to keep talking to both of them and not pick any sides. How could this happen? Everything was perfect and now it's ruined all over again! What could've happened that they wouldn't even talk to each other!?

I was devastated. I never fully understood what happened.

I got over it though and told them "This issue is between you two. I'm sorry, but I will still be friends with both of you. I'm not picking sides." They understood, but still wished I would side with one.

SUMMER SAYS BYE

Once I got back from my trip to California there was a back-to-school party that the whole group of girls got invited to. Of course I went and Hannah and Audrey were there, but something completely turned on inside Hannah and she left and wouldn't speak to me. I was so confused... what did I do? Was it something I said? I was so sad.

I relapsed. I thought I had been a good friend, and fair. Here I was, afraid again. I felt like I wasn't good enough and people would drop me like yesterday's garbage.

I couldn't stand the thought of it.

I started having nightmares and not sleeping well at night. Always afraid of something, even if I didn't know what. It was torture. I cried all the time, beating myself up for not being the best friend I could've been to Hannah. I turned off that inner warrior inside me and kept it all cooped up, and didn't let it out.

I started losing all the progress I had made with being self-assured and bold. I became this small person who didn't have a voice to speak up anymore.

A couple more months went by and I started thinking, what if I had confronted her about it? Then out of the blue, it hit me.

None of this was my fault.

I had been a great friend and she decided to shut me out and that was her not me. I didn't need to keep shrinking myself. It was time to release myself again.

I am fearless, and I will never stop.

THE END

Girls, be yourself. Don't be who everyone else is or who they think you should be.

It *will* pay off.

It will make people enjoy being around *you*. YOU can start being the leader. Be the bigger person in bad situations. It might be rough at first, but if you keep persisting it will make a difference.

We are the next generation and we need to start making a change in this world.
We can do it, we are **powerful** and **strong**.

We all have that inner warrior, sometimes we just need to let her out. Sometimes it just takes some encouragement. So come and join me on my journey to help girls across the nation find their inner soldier!
I really want to make a change, which is why I wrote this book. So if it made any difference to you, please share and tell your friends!

Come with me and be *Fearless!*

Fearless

ABOUT THE AUTHOR

Hi, I'm Mateja Mitchell. I'm outgoing, creative, tenacious, persuasive, kind, compassionate, empathetic, persistent, energetic, responsible, patient - and my friends say I'm funny, too! Haha.

I love horses and I love riding them. I love children too, and thank goodness, because I have five little sisters!

I'm proud of my accomplishments. I have overcome fear and what it can do, many times. I've stood up to people who could have potentially ruined some of my friendships, and I've discovered the amazing feeling and confidence that came from compassionately speaking what's in my heart and on my mind.

I'm now excited and proud to have unleashed my thoughts in a book to help others through some of their own challenges of childhood!

I hope my book *Fearless* encourages you to take control and overcome obstacles so that you can become fearless, too!

Please stay connected with me and share how this book helped you, by leaving me a **review on Amazon.com**.

I'd also love to connect on social media
www.Facebook.com/FearlessWeStand

Please help me grow this Fearless Empire at
www.FearlessWeStand.com

Stand Strong. Be You. Be Fearless!

63726250R00023

Made in the USA
Lexington, KY
16 May 2017